CW00538473

THE GREAT BOOK OF

rhubarb

ELAINE LEMM

GREAT N ORTHERN

Great Northern Books
PO Box 213, Ilkley, LS29 9WS
www.greatnorthernbooks.co.uk

ISBN: 978 1 905080 93 9

Design and layout: David Burrill

CIP Data
A catalogue for this book is available from the British Library

CONTENTS

Introduction

I have always liked rhubarb so when I was asked to write this book what I didn't expect was to fall in love with it. I knew vaguely of a history that had something to do with medicine and I was well aware that its culinary capacity was more than a pie or a crumble but what I hadn't realised until I began my research was the depth and breadth of each.

The journey of this humble, unassuming vegetable across thousands of years is fascinating, covers a huge swathe of the globe and in its pursuit, much conflict and a lot of money. All this for a rhubarb crumble? Not during this period. The chase was for the root and the medicinal benefits it offered and edible rhubarb only made its way into the kitchen a mere few hundred years ago. Initially this was in the form of pies and tarts with which we are more familiar, but in recent times is more often found in the hands of the chef. There are few foods around that can say as assuredly as rhubarb that they marry well with as many foods, or can be found in every part of a menu and store cupboard.

Falling in love with rhubarb!

My early memories of rhubarb are in the garden at home. The rhubarb plant was left to its own devices in the back corner and some time before Christmas was covered by an upturned dustbin to deprive the crown of light and to force thin, sweet stalks from the dormant plant. The arrival of this young rhubarb was always a highlight in the winter months.

I don't recall rhubarb served alongside meat or fish but I do remember my mother's rhubarb pie with delight, a huge slice with Bird's Custard - sorry chefs, crème anglaise does not work the same. A treat – though we children regarded it more of a dare – was dipping raw sticks of rhubarb into sugar and biting off huge chunks, which would have us hopping from foot to foot as the astringent juice burnt into our tongues and lips.

In the writing of the book more rhubarb has been cooked than I care to think about, and in every guise from sweet to savoury – in jams, chutneys, vodka, jellies and pies. It has been an extremely pleasurable journey for me alongside what is truly a jewel in the crown of foods and I hope you enjoy it as much as I have.

Elaine Lemm *July 2011*

Acknowledgements

As a Yorkshire lass, I have to give thanks to those who have worked so hard in the 'Rhubarb Triangle' of Leeds, Wakefield and Bradford to bring Yorkshire Forced Rhubarb onto the world stage. They work long and hard – and mainly in the dark – to cheer up our winter with their beautiful, forced rhubarb. Particular thanks to Janet and Neil Oldroyd Hulme, of Oldroyd's in Rothwell, one of Yorkshire's premier growers, for all their help in sharing their knowledge and expertise of all things rhubarb.

To my lovely stepdaughter Lucy, who at sixteen declared to me she would never cook but is now a cracker in the kitchen. A huge thank you for all your help in testing the recipes and your invaluable feedback from force feeding your partner Taylor and friends with the results.

To my editor David Joy, who again has guided me with patience and understanding through the daunting task of bringing a book together.

To Wendy and Yvonne, ruthless proof readers, and Irene for her help with research and arranging great interviews. Thank you girls.

And last but by no means the least to my husband Ron. Without your support nothing would get done, never mind writing a book about rhubarb. Promise not to feed you rhubarb again for a while!

What is Rhubarb?

Before we embark on the fascinating history, diverse uses and multiple recipes for rhubarb, I need to point out that rhubarb is classed as a vegetable here in the UK. I admit it does have an uncanny knack of appearing to be a fruit, is found in the fruit section of most supermarkets, and despite being a wonderful food companion to meat and fish is perhaps better known for its use in pies and puddings. In the US, however, it is a fruit, and was settled as such following a court ruling in 1947.

There are many types of rhubarb but they fall between the edible, the ornamental and the medicinal. Rheum Rhabarbarum – to give edible rhubarb its proper name – belongs to the botanical family Polygonaceae and as such is cousin to the sorrel. The name comes from a combination of the word Rha, the river in Siberia we now know as the Volga, and barbarum, the region of the Rha river inhabited by non-Romans also known as barbarians.

The ornamental varieties are particularly attractive, large plants, loved for their architectural value in the flower bed; rheum palmatum can grow up to five feet high with broad leaves and large crimson flowers. Chinese rhubarb is cultivated for the root which, when dried, is used for its medicinal qualities – but more of that later.

Edible rhubarb is a robust perennial and grown primarily for the stalks (petiole). The leaves of rhubarb, however, are poisonous, containing a high concentration of oxalic acid crystals. This acid is used widely in cleaning agents renowned for removing rust and ink stains, tanning leather and for cleaning the hull of boats. Consequently this is why it is a good idea not to eat rhubarb leaves though opinion is divided as to whether it is OK to compost the leaves.

The season for rhubarb spreads across most of the year, bar a few months. It starts late in the year when the first early-forced rhubarb appears in December – or early January depending on the weather. The season for the tender, sweet, stems continues through to March but then for a few weeks there is a lull until the hardier, robust field rhubarb becomes available from April to September.

The early, forced rhubarb is one of the treasures of the British food year. The glorious pinks and reds of the stem breathes lightness into heavy, winter cooking and for the cook it neatly fills the gap between the last of the native apples and the start of the soft fruit season in the spring.

Rhubarb, whether the early or summer variety, is one of the most versatile foods in the kitchen. Cooked together with sugar or honey it is an integral part of the great traditional British pudding, the acidic sharpness making it a perfect partner to oily fish and fatty meats. The colour enlivens a cordial or a home-made schnapps, and the robust flavour is an ideal component for a spicy chutney or relish.

Nutritional Info

Despite being 95% water, the remaining constituents are dietary fibre, potassium, magnesium, moderate levels of vitamin C and calcium – though the last when combined with oxalic acid is hard for the body to digest.

Forced rhubarb in former times – then as now
one of the treasures of the British food year.

A Brief History of Rhubarb

Much as rhubarb is considered an intrinsic part of British food, our claim to ownership goes back a mere few hundred years. It is millennia back and to Siberia we must go to find where it was originally cultivated. The first mention appears around 2700 BC in the Chinese herbal 'Pen King'. The dried root of Chinese rhubarb was an important medicinal drug, highly prized for its purgative qualities and for the treatment of many intestinal ailments, liver and gut problems.

Marco Polo is given credit for bringing the root to Europe in the 13th century but little is known of it in Britain until the 14th century when promises of purifying blood and making young wenches look fair captured the imagination. The route through to Europe came from different directions and the rhubarb that made it here by way of the Persian Gulf and the Red Sea was known as East Indian, whereas if it came by way of Persia and Syria it was Turkey Rhubarb.

In the 16th century, China first allowed Russia to trade on her frontiers and thus the first Chinese rhubarb came into Europe via Moscow. Russian rhubarb was good and therefore commanded a high price, with the Russian authorities keeping a watchful eye and control over the precious commodity. Demand for the miracle drug increased and new outlets were sought when China finally opened direct trade routes with Europe. This meant that by the mid 19th century Russian rhubarb had all but disappeared in Europe.

The price of rhubarb root commanded even more than opium, in France ten times the price of cinnamon, and four of saffron, which at the time was the most expensive spice in the world. It was a much-prized drug and the 'rabbit in the hat' for apothecaries and medics in their treatment of most ailments. Anyone who could unlock the key to the cultivation of the high quality Chinese root closer to home was set for fame and fortune. Throughout the 17th and 18th centuries this quest occupied British botanists, apothecaries, scientists and explorers. There were many failures but in 1777, Hayward, an apothecary in Banbury, Oxfordshire raised seed sent from Russia and produced roots of an outstanding quality. So successful was the cultivation it spread throughout neighbouring counties and into Yorkshire and still exists in Banbury today.

Likewise, Scotsman James Mounsey had been the doctor to tsar Peter III, but following his assassination fled for his life back to Lockerbie in Dumfriesshire. He brought rhubarb seeds with him and from these he also successfully grew fields of high quality rhubarb.

Throughout this time it was only the root which was sought after; the stalk and leaves were of no value and certainly not considered for any culinary merit. One paragraph, however, in a somewhat lengthy text between Englishman Peter Collinson and John Bantram in America – to whom Collinson had sent rhubarb seeds – speaks of Siberian rhubarb being the true sort (presumably to grow for root). He goes on to inform Collinson that this (Siberian) along with Rhapontic (another type of rhubarb) make excellent tarts:

'All you have to do is to take the stalks from the root, and from the leaves; peel off the rind and cut them in two or three pieces, and put them in crust with sugar and a little cinnamon; then bake the pie, or tart: eats best cold. It is much admired here, and has none of the effects the roots have. It eats most like gooseberry pie.'

Sounds familiar?

Engraved title page, showing a rhubarb plant with an oriental city and a palm tree in the background. From Mathias Tiling (1634-1685), Rhabarbarologia (Frankfurt, 1679).

Rhubarb inside the forcing sheds – a period scene.

That most industrious of food writers, Hannah Glasse, is attributed with what is believed to be one of the first recipes in print in 1760, thirteen years after her other famous 'first' – the recipe for Yorkshire Pudding.

Her recipe in the Compleat Confectioner is not dissimilar to that of Bantram and tells of taking the stalks of English rhubarb, cutting to the size of gooseberries, sweetening and making as you would a gooseberry tart. Frighteningly she adds at the end '… the leaves of rhubarb are a fine thing to eat for a pain in the stomach'. Anyone eating the poisonous leaves would certainly quickly forget about any pains in the stomach, I imagine.

Britain grabbed the culinary delights of rhubarb well before the rest of Europe. The falling price of sugar was certainly a contributing factor and soon pies, puddings, jams, jellies and wines made their way onto the British table.

However, a happy accident in the Chelsea Physic Garden in 1817 moved the enjoyment of rhubarb onto an entirely different level. In the depths of the winter a number of rhubarb roots were accidentally covered with soil by workmen digging a trench. Weeks later when the soil was removed, peeping through were tiny, tender, pink shoots of rhubarb that thankfully someone noticed. These shoots were noticeably better quality, had a far superior flavour and were less astringent than anything before. Soon commercial growers around London began blanching the rhubarb, with some also lifting the roots from the ground and into buildings to prevent disease, and by applying extra heat were able to harvest the rhubarb even earlier.

Further north in Yorkshire this method of bringing the rhubarb 'on' was taken onto a much larger scale. Huge sheds were erected to house the rhubarb and as the popularity of it grew, many in what became known as the 'Rhubarb Triangle' of Leeds, Wakefield and Bradford turned land over to the growing of it. Every weeknight during the intense short season trains carried up to 200 tons of the sweet, forced stems to the London markets.

The love affair with rhubarb continued through to the middle of the last century and then began to fade; there are many reasons given for it's demise. The second world war gets the brunt of the blame with a lack of sugar to sweeten the rhubarb; as nearly everyone had rhubarb in the garden it was readily available therefore eaten a lot and by the end of the war the nation was sick of it; and finally the land was needed for other crops. Rhubarb crowns for forcing need to be kept for three years without cropping but in wartime this waste was deemed immoral, so the crowns were cropped and pulped into jam. As a treat, children were given a stick of rhubarb and a little sugar into which to dip it, and when sweets finally made it back children certainly did not want to eat rhubarb.

Post war and eventually the end of rationing also saw the arrival of newer, chic fruits and vegetables, making poor old rhubarb seem a little old fashioned.

Now in the 21st century, rhubarb is back. After years of eating foreign, imported foods, attention has once again turned to the home grown. The increasing awareness of where our foods originate and questions on the impact on the environment of importing foods means provenance, seasonality and locality are paramount in choosing the foods we eat. Rhubarb is a major beneficiary of this exposure and is flourishing. It is once again the darling of celebrity chefs and home cooks alike. It has gained the lofty status of a 'superfood' and, just as with the Chinese millennia, rhubarb has seized the attention of medical studies owing to certain properties which are causing great excitement in the area of cancer research.

Yorkshire Rhubarb

The happy accident in the physic garden at Chelsea in 1817 – when rhubarb crowns accidentally covered with soil revealed a way of growing rhubarb that resulted in a sweeter, more tender and less astringent stalk – also had a huge impact in Yorkshire two hundred miles further north. Rhubarb was already grown in Yorkshire at this time, but it was the outdoor, hardy crowns used mainly for medicinal purposes. The discovery of forcing the crowns into early production by blanching – depriving the crowns of light – was taken up in Yorkshire, predominantly by the Whitwell family in the Kirkstall area of Leeds. They became the major challengers to the London growers, and it was here that the first purpose-built sheds were erected for forcing rhubarb.

What had started as a haphazard process was further developed in these carefully controlled environments and the number of growers rapidly increased to over two hundred. The 'Rhubarb Triangle' formed between Leeds, Bradford and Wakefield in the then West Riding was born and went on to become the centre of the world's production of forced rhubarb.

Why the West Riding ?

As the origins of rhubarb are Siberian then obviously it loves a cold climate and it also needs a lot of water and a good supply of nitrogen. The part of the West Riding now known as West Yorkshire is located close to the Pennines, the hilly backbone of Britain. The shadow of these hills creates not only a frost pocket but also a high level of rainfall, which provided invaluable water to the rhubarb growers. Leeds and the surrounding area was also the centre of the world's woollen industry at this time. Woollen waste, which was of no use to them, or waste from nearby shoddy mills, was valuable to the rhubarb growers. The fields were fertilised with the fibres, which as they were broken down

When Yorkshire led the World!
– a forced rhubarb display board.

provided a priceless source of nitrogen.

Coal for heating the sheds was plentiful with the rich Yorkshire coalfields close by, and with coal, wool and now rhubarb to export from the county, Yorkshire was at the crossroads of the rail network. The nightly 'Rhubarb Express' from Yorkshire would rapidly deliver the freshly harvested stalks to the London markets, from where they went onto Europe every night during the short, intense three month season. At the peak of the season this was as much as two hundred tons a day.

With so many of forced rhubarb's necessities in one place, how could it fail? It didn't and went on to enjoy almost a whole century of success.

The post-war decline in rhubarb's popularity severely affected the growers in Yorkshire. What had been two hundred growers shrank to only eleven; the thousands of acres given over to rhubarb shrivelled to around four hundred, and the 'Rhubarb Express' ceased its nightly journey in the mid 1960s.

The revival of rhubarb came on the back of the revival of interest in and desire for indigenous, locally grown produce. A highly publicised, and ultimately successful, campaign to protect the traditionally grown rhubarb under the European PDO (Protected Designation of Origin) status has put Yorkshire rhubarb back on the world stage. The Yorkshire growers were led, by among others, Janet Oldroyd Hulme, of E H Oldroyd & Sons, rhubarb growers for five generations. They mounted a vigorous campaign to raise awareness of the uniqueness of Yorkshire rhubarb and the need to protect the name from the deluge of foreign imports imitating the forcing method. Once awarded, no-one else can call their rhubarb Yorkshire Forced, and only rhubarb grown in the designated triangle has the right to be so called. For the consumer it means that when buying Yorkshire Forced Rhubarb they can be assured it is of the expected quality and flavour and grown in the traditional manner.

It was a lengthy battle to be awarded the designation and the

Good times for forced rhubarb with a special display at Selfridges in London.

winning of it means not only worldwide recognition but a massive boost in sales.

Inside the Forcing Sheds

The purpose-built sheds for forcing rhubarb are exactly as described – huge sheds. They are completely dark save for the candlelight, which, contrary to belief, is not for the rhubarb to grow but for the pickers to be able to see what they are doing. Any light will start the process of photosynthesis so the area around the candles is cleaned of rhubarb and when there is no-one in the sheds, the candles are extinguished.

Two to three year old rhubarb roots are first lifted from the fields

Miaora Popa checks the rhubarb under candlelight at E H Oldroyd & Sons, near Leeds.

only after they have been exposed to frost and are then planted in the sheds. These roots have never had a crop taken from them as they are grown specifically for forcing. By not cropping the root all the energy is retained, stored in the root and only used when the forcing process begins. The forcing unfortunately eventually kills the plants, so each year they must be replaced.

Once in the sheds the plant is deprived of light and of food, which 'forces' the root to begin growing the rhubarb stalks. It grows quickly, so quickly that it is possible if it is quiet in the shed to hear the 'popping' sound as the stalks are pushed out from the bud.

The rhubarb must be harvested by hand, a time-consuming process as each stem must be removed intact from the root. The stick is ready to be picked when it is an arm's length long, then

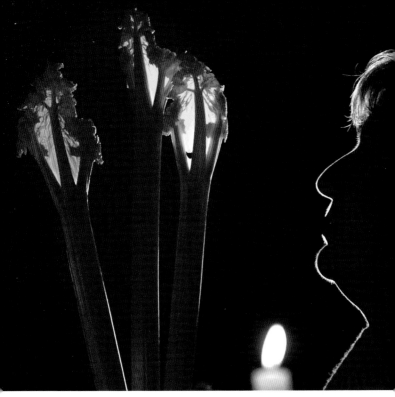

Janet Oldroyd checks some of her rhubarb at her farm.

the picker inserts a finger between the stick and bud at the base, gently pushing whilst twisting and pulling. Any remnant of stalk left in the bud could rot and potentially cause botrytis, a fungus which can quickly spread and affect the whole shed – a disaster for any rhubarb grower.

Questions have been asked by visitors to the sheds if it is in fact cruel to deprive the rhubarb plants of light and food. I have been assured by Janet Oldroyd-Hulme that this is not the case. She tells me that she has never heard the plants scream.

Medicinal Benefits

Culinary Rhubarb and Cancer

Despite its illustrious history, rhubarb has also suffered as the stuff of childhood ridicule linking it to 'nonsense or rubbish'. Stewed rhubarb and lumpy custard of school dinner days didn't do it many favours either, but change has been on the cards for some time. It is back in favour with both the public and chefs alike as each pursues the desire for locally-sourced, traditional foods.

Researchers from Sheffield Hallam University and the Dundee-based Scottish Crop Research Institute (SCRI) have now found that baking British common garden rhubarb for just twenty minutes dramatically increased levels of chemicals, called polyphenols – anti-cancer chemicals. The researchers cooked the rhubarb four different ways by blanching, slow cooking, fast cooking and baking it and found that, apart from the blanching, this led to an increase in polyphenol content. Fortunately, these are the most common ways to cook rhubarb, with slow roasting a particular favourite as it keeps both the colour, shape and flavour.

Dr Gordon McDougall, from SCRI's Plant Products and Food Quality programme says: "The main thing we discovered is that rhubarb in Britain has anti-cancer and bioactive components. Our research has shown it is a potential source of pharmacological agents that may be used to develop anti-cancer drugs. We have also shown that the levels of these anti-cancer and bioactive components increase if you cook it in a certain way. Baking was the most gentle, in that it didn't destroy those components but released them from the material."

This was the first time research had been carried out on the culinary variety. Previously it had centred around oriental rhubarb, which for centuries has been recognised for its health benefits and has been used in traditional Chinese medicine for thousands of years.

Fresh Rhubarb

Fresh rhubarb stalk is a good source of dietary fibre and beneficial for those suffering from indigestion. Eating a cold piece of rhubarb stalk can help counterbalance stomach acid and eating fresh rhubarb regularly has been seen to have a positive effect on lowering of blood pressure. Rhubarb has been found to have anti-oxidant, anti-inflammatory and anti-allergy properties.

Rhubarb Root

Rhubarb is one of the most widely-used herbs in Chinese medicine. Six-year old roots are harvested in the autumn and dried. In measured doses, rhubarb root works as a mild laxative, is a tonic for the digestive system, helps ease chronic constipation, and equally soothes diarrhoea. It calms the liver and gall bladder, reduces certain menopausal symptoms such as hot flushes, and is effective for haemorrhoids. According to the Rhubarb Compendium, people have claimed that rhubarb enhances the appetite when taken in small amounts before meals, it also promotes blood circulation and relieves pain in cases of injury or inflammation, inhibits intestinal infections and can also reduce auto-immune reactions.

Phew!

Rhubarb root should never be used by pregnant or nursing women.

Not just a Vegetable
– Other Uses for Rhubarb

The leaves

Rhubarb leaves are poisonous due to a high concentration of oxalic acid crystals. Once extracted this acid is used as:

A cleaning agent, particularly good for removing ink and rust stains and is used widely in products for cleaning boat hulls.

Tanning leather.

The strained liqueur created from boiling rhubarb leaves and adding soap flakes makes an effective insecticide against leaf-eating insects.

The rhubarb stalks

Used widely as a natural dye including recently on the roof of the velodrome built for the 2012 Olympics. London Mayor Boris Johnson personally thanked the designers for boosting the British rhubarb industry.

"The secret to that rosy hue is that it is achieved by rubbing it with rhubarb," he said after admiring the venue's red cedar cladding at the official opening. "It is lovingly rubbed with rhubarb."

Also used as:

A natural hair dye for blond or light brown hair.

Cleaning pans – rub the rhubarb over stubborn stains or onto burnt on food and hey presto!

Rhubarb fibres make a lovely addition to hand-made papers.

Rhubarb in the Garden

It is hardly surprising that once upon a time, and not that long ago, almost every garden or allotment had rhubarb growing as it is one of the easiest plants to cultivate. I have clear memories of my father's plants tucked under an upturned dustbin at the bottom of the garden. As kids we loved to whip away the dustbin and snap off a pink, juicy stalk, which we dipped into sugar and ate like a Sherbert Dip. It never crossed our minds to wash the rhubarb before we ate it, but Dad never used chemicals and the most help the rhubarb had was a hefty dose of horse manure around the root.

When rhubarb fell out of favour in the 1960s and '70s many but not all of the crowns were grubbed up. I have a friend who is successfully still growing rhubarb from a crown now believed to be over a hundred years old.

The recent renaissance of the vegetable, however, means rhubarb is back growing happily in the British garden and allotment. Nurseries and garden centres are selling crowns, with one – Brandy Carr in Yorkshire – holding one of the largest collections of rhubarb varieties, both culinary and ornamental. There are at least a hundred varieties from which to choose, though some of the rarer may not always be available.

If you thought that all rhubarb was the same – a long red-pinkish or green stalk with large fan-like green leaves as seen on the supermarket shelves – then it may be worth a visit to view one of Britain's gardens housing a rhubarb collection. There are several significant collections in the UK but two of the better known belong to the Royal Horticultural Society. There is also the beautiful kitchen garden at the National Trust's Clumber Park in north Nottinghamshire.

The Royal Horticultural Society
– Wisley and Harlow Carr, Harrogate

Non-ornamental rhubarb collections have been held at RHS garden at Wisley since 1904 and at one time included over a hundred cultivars, including some of historical interest. Currently their horticultural database lists over 270 species and additionally a full photographic record of the collection is being built up. Along with descriptions and drawings of stem cross-sections it is hoped this will provide valuable information for identifying various cultivars.

At RHS Harlow Carr in Harrogate there is a substantial collection of over seventy per cent of all the named varieties of rhubarb, and many are Yorkshire bred. The collection of predominantly edible plants was for many years hidden from view, as it was felt there was no longer much interest in the plant. Plus, given the amount of space an outdoor variety can take up once it reaches full-size in mid-summer, it was thought the garden would benefit from more 'popular' plants.

As the interest in rhubarb once again flourished it was time to bring it out of exile and back to its rightful place in the vegetable garden. In the winter of 2010 large beds were prepared for a spring planting. Most of the newly planted crowns adapted quickly to their new home and are flourishing. A few are taking a little longer, but overall the new beds have been deemed a great success by RHS kitchen gardener Amy Lax, with a lot of interest from visitors to the garden . As the plants take time to grow and fill the space given over to them, Amy has planted between with the herb Sweet Cicely. It not only looks pretty but is a delicious herb to include in a rhubarb recipe as it imparts a warm, gentle aniseed flavour to the dish.

Clumber Park – North Nottinghamshire

Though over 65 miles south of Harlow Carr, there are strong links between the RHS garden and the kitchen garden at Clumber Park – the 3,800 acres of green open space in North Nottinghamshire owned by the National Trust. Clumber has one of England's finest walled kitchen gardens with magnificent 400 foot herbaceous borders, heritage varieties of fruit trees and a 450 foot long-range glasshouse.

Head gardener at Clumber is Chris Margrave, who previously was head gardener at Harlow where he had established the National Rhubarb Collection long before the garden was owned by the RHS. Chris is a self-confessed rhubarb enthusiast, which he attributes to having grown up in Wakefield, part of the Rhubarb Triangle. His impetus in creating the collection came from his awareness of the diminishing rhubarb industry around his home town.

When Harlow Carr let it be known they were looking for a garden to help with some of the older and endangered species, Chris quite naturally jumped at the chance. There were already thirty varieties in the garden and sixty were then added from Harlow, all of which are edible. The collection varies from endangered and rare early, mid and late varieties through to new varieties. Many of these were developed at Stockbridge House, near Selby, in the 1960s and '70s, where research was carried out to produce more robust, commercial varieties.

The planting of the walled garden is much as it would have originally been when it would have supplied the 'big house'. The planting was done to be able to create a year-round supply of fruits, vegetables and flowers. Rhubarb was useful in this planting, as it would grow happily in the north facing part of the garden where less robust vegetables would not survive.

Rooting among the rhubarb beds at Clumber is a fascinating experience as it quickly becomes apparent how different one stick of rhubarb is alongside another. Chris takes account of all of the

New rhubarb beds at the Royal Horticultural Society, Harlow Carr, Harrogate.

Head gardener Chris Margrave checking Timperley Early rhubarb in the walled kitchen garden at Clumber Park, near Worksop.

following to help identify the various varieties:

- Colour of the stalk

- Colour of the flesh

- Thickness of the stalk

- Some stalks are flat on one edge, some are concave.

- Stalks can be smooth and some ridged

- Leaf size

- Leaf shape

- Leaf colour

- Leaf margin

Flavour will also help in identification and Chris explains this can vary from hints of cherry and greengage to apple and strawberry. Some will be sweeter, some more astringent. With so many differences to take into account it is not surprising there are so many varieties. It is Chris's ambition not only to save the endangered species but he is also looking to apply for National Collection status as soon as he has the required three crowns for each variety.

Other places to see Rhubarb in the UK

There are many stately home gardens, walled gardens and farms growing rhubarb. Check with your local tourist office. Here are a few different types of visits to see rhubarb in its many guises:

The Eden Project is a top garden and eco visitor attraction in Cornwall with Rainforest and Mediterranean Biomes. They have a small collection of rhubarb plants in the Dye Garden alongside other plants used traditionally for dying fabrics and wools.

The Alnwick Garden project began just ten years ago. It is now a vibrant place, with beautifully landscaped gardens, magnificent architecture and unique features, all brought to life with water. Part of the gardens is the Poison Garden, which features many plants grown unwittingly in back gardens, and those that grow in the British countryside, as well as many more unusual varieties including rhubarb, the leaves of which are poisonous.

Rhubarb Tours

Oldroyd's are one of the main growers of Yorkshire forced rhubarb and every season offer the chance to learn more about this wonderful industry and to visit the candlelight forcing sheds.

The visit starts with refreshments followed by a talk on the ancient history of rhubarb, how and why it was used as a medicine, how we came to eat rhubarb, and how the forcing process was discovered. There is then a fascinating tour of the forcing sheds to discuss the process and how it works.

Growing Rhubarb

There really isn't an easier plant to grow than rhubarb. It doesn't suffer too much from neglect and asks for little other than a good feed and plenty of water. The beauty of rhubarb is that it will thrive quiet happily in a partially shady corner and will provide you with fresh, vibrant stalks at a time when there is little else in the garden.

Here are a few tips from the experts:

- The soil should be prepared well in advance of planting, at least four weeks ahead or, if possible, the season before. The soil should be cleared of stones and as much organic matter dug into it as possible. Rhubarb is a hungry plant and likes to be well fed.

- Though rhubarb can be grown from seed, experts recommend growing from plants bought at a reputable nursery, or better still, ask a friend who already has a plant to divide it, preferably in the winter. If buying a plant, buy a year-old crown and make sure it is strong and disease free.

- Plant preferably in the late autumn or early winter. Bear in mind that outdoor plants grow vigorously and like plenty of room. Make sure there is space and that once fully grown, it won't be shading other plants.

- Plant so the top of the crown is at, or slightly above, soil level and space from 75cm up to 120 cm depending on the variety. Mulch with a layer of organic compost.

- Always make sure the plants have plenty of water, especially in hot weather and feed well in the autumn once the plants stop growing.

Young rhubarb crowns.

- Divide the crowns every five or six years.

- You should wait at least one season before harvesting any stalks.

- The flower shoots on edible varieties should always be removed.

If you want to force the rhubarb for the slender, sweeter stalks early in the year, as soon as the plant shows new shoots in the winter, cover with a large bucket or container to cut out all the light. Keep checking and harvest when the stalks are long and erect.

And a final word from Chris Margarve:

"Rhubarb looks after itself, plant it and walk away, it's that easy."

Thanks to Chris Margrave at Clumber Park and Amy Lax at Harlow Carr Gardens for their tips.

Pot of young rhubarb.

Monty Python – The Rhubarb Tart Song

I want another slice of rhubarb tart.
I want another lovely slice.
I'm not disparaging the blueberry pie
But rhubarb tart is oh so very nice.
A rhubarb what? A rhubarb tart!
A whatbarb tart? A rhubarb tart!
I want another slice of rhubarb tart!

The principles of modern philosophy
Were postulated by Descartes.
Discarding everything he wasn't certain of
He said 'I think therefore I am a rhubarb tart.'
A rhubarb what? A rhubarb tart!
A Rene who? Rene Descartes!
Poor nut he thought he was a rhubarb tart!

Read all the existentialist philosophers,

Like Schopenhauer and Jean-Paul Sartre.

Even Martin Heidegger agrees on one thing:

Eternal happiness is rhubarb tart.

A rhubarb what? A rhubarb tart!

A Jean-Paul who? A Jean-Paul Sartre!

Eternal happiness is rhubarb tart.

A rhubarb tart has fascinated all the poets.

Especially the immortal bard.

He caused Richard the Third to call on Bosworth Field:

'My kingdom for a slice of rhubarb tart!'

A rhubarb what? A rhubarb bard!

Immortal what? Immortal tart!

As rhymes go that is really pretty bard!

I want another slice of rhubarb tart

I want another lovely slice

I'm not disparaging the blueberry pie

But rhubarb tart is oh-so-very nice.

Rhubarb Crumble and Custard Garden

In the late spring of 2010, the official tourism body Welcome to Yorkshire, won a silver medal at the prestigious Chelsea Flower Show in London for its Rhubarb Crumble and Custard Garden. The garden itself is a quirky take on the classic dish, inspired by Yorkshire's own rhubarb triangle, featuring an overflowing bowl of rhubarb crumble and custard and a giant wooden spoon. Royal Horticultural Society judges recognised that the courtyard garden, which celebrates the best in Yorkshire produce and craftmanship, was worthy of the prestigious award. The garden is now in permanent residence at RHS Harlow Carr, Harrogate.

Rhubarb in the Kitchen

There is no doubt as to the efficacy of rhubarb root as a medicine – history through to modern-day research is showing that its use in this field is only set to grow. But most of us are more familiar with rhubarb in the kitchen. Without doubt rhubarb is one of the most versatile foods in the hands of a cook or chef. It can be stewed, roasted, baked or boiled. It is as happy as a comforting, stodgy pudding as it is in a sophisticated jelly. It plays nicely with fatty meats and oily fish, makes a delicious jam or partner to hot spices and exotic fruits in a chutney or relish. Watch it turn from vegetable to wine, add a glow to vodka or a blush to a summer cordial. How many other vegetables do you know that can do that?

Choosing and Storing Rhubarb

Forced rhubarb comes in all shades of pink through to dark red, depending on the variety. The main season, outdoor rhubarb will vary from a pink-green mixture to all green. Whatever the type or colour, it should be vibrant and fresh looking. The rhubarb stalks of all varieties should be firm and upright. The leaves (if still present) of forced rhubarb should be a pale yellow, and if main season a perky green – neither should ever be black.

As with all local, seasonal foods, rhubarb is best eaten fresh. Avoid storing rhubarb for too long but if you need to store it, place it in a cool, dark place or in the vegetable drawer of the refrigerator.

Rhubarb freezes very well and can be kept frozen for up to six months. If you don't know how you may want to cook the rhubarb later simply cut the stalks into pieces, open freeze on a tray and once frozen place into freezer bags. If you want to use the rhubarb in sweet dishes, place the chopped rhubarb into freezer bags, add a tablespoon of granulated sugar, give the bag a good shake, seal the bags and freeze. Or, precook the rhubarb by cutting the rhubarb stalks into small pieces and poach gently, three or four minutes, in a little sugared water. Cool and freeze. This simple rhubarb compote can be used in pies and crumbles, folded into custard and whipped cream or in many other recipes.

Forced rhubarb will never need peeling as it is already tender. Stalks of main crop sometimes need a little light peeling, later in the season it may need stripping completely; one way to tell is to snap a stalk to see how fibrous are the outer fibres.

There are numerous varieties of culinary rhubarb available to the gardener, including some heritage and rare plants. For the consumer, we have to rely on the varieties popular with commercial growers.

Favourite Culinary Varieties

Cawood Delight – an outdoor variety with the beautiful colour of a forced. Excellent for cooking.

Crimson Red – has a sharp distinctive, but sweet, flavour.

Champagne – can be forced to provide sticks as early as February and can be grown outdoors as well.

Queen Victoria – an older variety still loved for its heavy yields and good flavour.

Reeds Early Superb – a lovely dark colour when forced, with a distinctive earthy flavour.

Stockbridge Arrow – a high yielding, modern, main crop variety with excellent colour and flavour. Easily distinguished in the forcing shed by the arrowhead shaped leaf.

Stockbridge Harbinger – is a beautiful, dark red colour when forced. More difficult to grow than other varieties.

Sutton – was introduced by Suttons Seeds in 1893 and remains a tasty choice.

Timperley Early – a very popular variety for its early cropping and good flavour.

Valentine – has tender rose-coloured stalks, with a wonderful flavour, perfect for pies or jams.

Victoria – an old reliable variety that varies in size.

Zwolle seedling – has good flavour and fragrance, and stays firm when cooked.

Roasted Rhubarb

Quite often rhubarb is stewed for use in various rhubarb recipes, or recipes using rhubarb. A delicious alternative is to roast the rhubarb in the oven with a little orange juice and brown sugar. This roasting helps the rhubarb to keep its beautiful colour, it intensifies the flavour and retains the shape of the rhubarb rather than a mush. Once you have your roasted rhubarb, use as you would in any recipe with stewed rhubarb or freeze.

450g rhubarb
2 tbsp soft brown sugar
3 tbsp orange juice

Preheat the oven to 350°F/175°C/Gas 4.

Cut the rhubarb into 1in/3cm pieces. Place the rhubarb into an ovenproof dish. Sprinkle over the sugar and the orange juice.

Loosely cover the dish with tin foil, a lid or simply a roasting tray. Bake in the preheated oven for approx 20 minutes or until the rhubarb is cooked through but not falling apart.

Rhubarb ready for roasting.

Simple Stewed Rhubarb

Cooking most certainly doesn't get easier than this. Simple stewed rhubarb is so easy and quick. Use young forced, or summer outdoor rhubarb, it doesn't matter. Once stewed, the rhubarb can be used in many different recipes. It also freezes well, so if you have a glut, cook it and pop it in the freezer. To ring the changes, add a little piece if fresh ginger if liked.

750g rhubarb, washed and trimmed
Juice of 1 large orange
100g caster sugar

Using a non-aluminium pan, place the rhubarb with the orange juice and sugar. Bring to a gentle boil, turn the heat down and simmer until the rhubarb is soft but not completely collapsed.

Taste and adjust the sweetness to your liking.

Rhubarb in Film

Rhubarb was a 1969 British short film written and directed by Eric Sykes, starring Sykes and Harry Secombe. The dialogue consisted entirely of repetitions of the word 'rhubarb'. All the characters' last names were 'Rhubarb', and even the licence plates on vehicles were 'RHU BAR B'. A baby 'spoke' by holding a sign with the word 'Rhubarb' written on it.
Rhubarb is a 1951 film adapted from the 1946 novel *Rhubarb* by humorist H. Allen Smith, where a rich eccentric bequeaths ownership of a baseball team to a cat named Rhubarb.

SAVOURY

Polish Rhubarb Soup

Rhubarb is plentiful in Poland, and finding it in a soup is not uncommon. In the heat of late spring and early summer, cold rhubarb soup was a refreshing noontime meal for the farmers returning from the fields.

This recipe comes from Barbara Rolex, Expert Food Writer of the About Eastern European Food web site.

Serves 4

    450g rhubarb, trimmed, peeled, if necessary, and chopped
    1.2 litres water
    2 tbsp cornflour
    120 ml whole milk
    1 tbsp seedless strawberry preserves
    Sugar to taste
    Cooked 'kluski' egg noodles or croutons
    Sour cream for garnish

Place rhubarb and water in large pot. Bring to boil, reduce heat and simmer until rhubarb is tender, about 15 minutes. Remove pot from heat. Purée with a hand blender or in a conventional blender or food processor.

Dissolve cornflour in milk, then slowly whisk into hot soup. Add strawberry preserves to improve the soup's colour (or add a drop of red food colouring) and sweeten to taste with sugar. Return to heat, bring to a boil and simmer for three minutes.

Chill soup in an ice bath and refrigerate until ready to serve. Portion 'kluski' (or croutons) into bowls, ladle soup over and add a dollop of sour cream.

Spiced Braised Pork with Rhubarb

Pork is such a wonderful meat and one of my favourite cooking methods is braising. This Braised Pork recipe combines the pork with rhubarb, a delicious accompaniment to any fatty meat.

This pork recipe produces lots of juices which make a lovely sauce.

My other love of this braised pork recipe is its versatility. The cooked pork is delicious served with vegetables, the cold pork is lovely pulled from the bone and made into a salad, or a cold, spicy pork sandwich.

Serves 4 as a main course

> 1.5 kg pork shoulder, on the bone
> 4 large shallots, peeled
> 6 garlic cloves, peeled
> 2in/5cm fresh ginger, peeled and grated
> 3 tbsp honey
> 1 tsp freshly ground pepper
> 2 tbsp extra virgin olive oil
> 2 red chillies
> 500ml dry cider
> 500g rhubarb, trimmed weight
> 1 tsp ice cold butter, chopped into tiny pieces

Preheat the oven to 180°C/350°F/ Gas 4.

Score the skin of the pork with a very sharp knife then put into a large, roomy roasting tray. Put the shallots, garlic, ginger, honey, pepper and olive oil into a food processor and blitz to form a thick paste. Smear the paste all over the pork – skin and meat included.

Snap the chillies to open them slightly and throw into the roasting tray and pour in the cider. Cover tightly with aluminium foil and roast in the preheated oven for 2 hours.

Take the dish from the oven and increase the temperature to 220°C/Gas7. Remove the foil and baste the pork with the pan juices. Cut the rhubarb into 7cm lengths and scatter into the sauce. Return the tray to the oven, uncovered, for 20 minutes or until well coloured.

Remove the pork from the oven and place to one side to rest for at least 10 minutes before slicing.

Strain the pan juices through a fine sieve into a small saucepan. Keep the rhubarb to one side.

Place the sauce over a high heat and reduce by one third. Drop a few pieces of the ice cold butter into the sauce and and over a medium heat shake until all the butter has melted, repeat until all the butter is used up and the sauce is shiny and glossy.

Slice the pork (it will not make neat slices but don't worry, this is a quite rustic dish), place on a serving plate topped with the rhubarb and serve with the sauce.

Serve with slow-roasted or fresh seasonal vegetables. The pork is also lovely cold pulled from the bone and made into a salad or a sandwich.

Spiced Braised Pork with Rhubarb.

Ham Hock and Moss House Rhubarb Terrine

Recipe from Rudding Park Hotel, Harrogate

Serves 6

1 ham hock	50g dried prunes, chopped
1 chopped carrot	10g tarragon, chopped
¼ head of celery, chopped	10g parsley, chopped
1 onion, chopped	50g Yorkshire rhubarb
1 bay leaf	80ml reduced beef stock
2 cloves	1litre water
1 shallot, finely chopped	500g sugar
50g dried apricots, chopped	

Preparing the rhubarb:

Peel the rhubarb and cut into batons of 5cm length, then cut the batons in three length wise. Place the sugar and the water in a saucepan and bring to the boil. Put in the rhubarb batons and cook for 30 seconds, remove the batons from the syrup and cool down. Reserve in the fridge.

Cooking the ham hocks:

Before cooking the ham hock you need to soak it in water for a couple of hours to eliminate the excess of salt and impurities from the meat.

Once soaked, rinse the ham hock under the cold water tap and place it in a large saucepan, then cover with water. Add the chopped carrot, onion, celery, bay leaf and cloves, and boil on medium heat for two hours or until the meat falls off the bone, always making sure the ham is covered with water. If necessary, add more water.

Once cooked, take the ham hock out of the water and leave to cool. Once cooled, finely pick the meat off the bone and place in a large bowl.

Making the terrine mix:

Add the chopped shallot, apricot, prunes, herbs and the beef stock to the meat and mix well.

On your kitchen worktop, place a 40cm long layer of cling film. Double that layer by adding another layer over the top (doubling the layer of cling film will make it a lot easier to handle and roll).

Place half of your terrine mix lengthwise in the middle of the sheet of cling film, then apply the rhubarb batons over the top. Add the other half of terrine mix over the top of the rhubarb, fold the cling film over the top, grab each end and roll tight into a sausage shape. Twist the ends to seal.

Reserve the terrine in the fridge for a couple of hours to set.

Once set your terrine is ready to slice. The terrine can be served with salad leaves, toasted bread and chutney.

Rarbarber Meets Rhubarb
Rhubarb is loved around the world and to prove the point here is the word 'rhubarb' in 22 other languages.

Arabic - rawand
Bulgarian - reven
Catalan - ruibarbe
Danish - rabarber
Dutch - rabarber
Finnish - raparperi
French - rhubarbe
German - rhabarber
Greek - reon
Hebrew - ribas
Hungarian - rebarbarabor
Italian - rabarbaro

Japanese - daio
Norwegian - rabarbra
Persian - riwand
Polish - rabarbar
Portuguese - ruibarbo
Romanian - rubarbura
Russian - reven
Serbo-Croat - rabarbara
Spanish - ruibarbo
Swedish - rabarber
Turksish - ravent

Rhubarb Avant-garde

Rob Green, *Green's Restaurant, Whitby:*

Memories of rhubarb for me were not particularly a great experience. Dad looked after the rhubarb patch with great passion, while Mum (god bless her) made a hash of it in the kitchen, in the form of a stodgy, sour 'crumble'.

Suffice to say, even as a young trainee chef, rhubarb held little culinary desire for me. If it was present in the kitchen, whilst head chef was away, it was strapped around my legs emulating cricket pads. French baguette in hand, the kitchen porter would bowl a vine tomato 'Yorker' at me. I never did hit a six.

Thankfully times have moved on. My first real experience of rhubarb was when I moved to Yorkshire some twenty years ago and became aware of the fantastic rhubarb triangle. Since then I have been a keen lover and every season it is a firm favourite with me, my chefs and our customers at Green's.

Rhubarb is a great match with mackerel, which being an oily fish works well with sweet and sour combinations. The addition of the ginger, orange, star anise and sesame seeds all work with the rhubarb and give this dish recipe an oriental feel.

Pan-fried Whitby Mackerel with a Ginger and Orange Potato Salad, Toasted Sesame Seeds, Sweet & Sour Rhubarb Sauce

Serves 4 as a starter

12 new potatoes, washed, cooked, cooled, sliced into 1 cm pieces
4 oranges, zest of half an orange
1 tbsp of fresh finely chopped ginger, blanched and refreshed three times

1 tbsp extra virgin olive oil
Sea salt and fresh ground black pepper
1 medium onion, chopped finely
25g butter
6 vine tomatoes, quartered
500g rhubarb, trimmed into 2cm pieces
1 tbsp honey
1 tablespoon tomato purée
1 whole star anise
4 fillets of fresh mackerel, pin bones removed
2 tsp of sesame seeds, dry roasted in a frying pan

The salad: In a mixing bowl, place the potatoes, juice of one orange, zest of half an orange, half the ginger, the olive oil and a good grind of sea salt and black pepper. Gently toss the mixture until the potatoes are coated. Cover and set aside at room temperature.

The sauce: Sauté the onion with the butter over a medium heat until soft and just starting to caramelise. Add the vine tomatoes and rhubarb and cook until soft. Juice the remaining oranges and add the juice along with the honey, remaining ginger, tomato purée and the star anise.

Simmer on a low heat for 20 minutes, remove the star anise and purée with a hand blender. Pass through a fine sieve and correct the seasoning. Keep warm.

The fish: Lightly dust the fillets in seasoned flour and pan fry in a little oil, skin side down first, for 2 – 3 minutes (depending on the size of your fillets) then flip over and finish for just 30 seconds on the flesh side. Place the fillets on kitchen paper in a warm place.

Discard any excess marinade from the potatoes and arrange in the centre of a warm plate. Place a fillet of mackerel on top of the potato salad. Sprinkle with the sesame seeds and spoon the sauce around the fish. Garnish with a few baby herbs.

Chicken Tikka with Rhubarb Mayonnaise

An unusual and intriguing recipe from Leeds schoolteacher, Linda Oldroyd. The Food and Drink programme on BBC set up a rhubarb recipe competition and Linda was asked to teach wine expert and presenter Oz Clarke how to cook with rhubarb. Oz then entered the competition with this recipe and called it Rhubarb Razzmatazz. He did not win but Linda did get full marks in each of the marking categories. The recipe works best with and was devised for forced rhubarb as opposed to outdoor grown.

Serves 4

400g forced rhubarb
100g caster sugar

Mayonnaise ingredients
4 heaped tbsp mayonnaise
1 heaped tbsp rhubarb or mango chutney
1 rounded tsp tikka paste
4 heaped tbsp rhubarb puree
Freshly milled salt and pepper
¼ cucumber, finely diced

2 sticks celery, finely diced
200g chilled, cooked chicken pieces (roughly chopped)

Garnish
1 packet of watercress or mixed salad leaves
Zest of an orange
Thinly sliced red onion rings

Set the oven to 175°C/350°F/Gas 5.

Wipe rhubarb and chop into 2.5cm/1in chunks. Place rhubarb in a large flat dish and sprinkle over a tablespoon of water and the sugar. Cover with foil and bake for 20 - 25 minutes. The rhubarb should be tender but retaining shape. Reserve about 16 pieces of rhubarb, discard the juice and purée the remaining pieces.

Combine all ingredients for the mayonnaise adding the cooked chicken last. Pile onto a bed of watercress or salad leaves and garnish with the reserved chunks of rhubarb, orange zest and onion rings.

Potted Duck with Rhubarb

from Chef Lionel Strub

Lionel is chef-owner of Mirabelle Restaurant, Harrogate. He was born and brought up in the Alsace region of France but has lived and worked in the UK for many years. His recipe brings together ingredients from both countries.

Serves 4

200g pork belly, diced
3 duck legs
200ml white wine
2 garlic cloves whole
1tbsp mustard seeds, crushed

Sea salt & freshly ground pepper
250g rhubarb trimmed and cut into cubes

Pre heat the oven to 160°C/325°F/Gas 3.

Place the pork and the duck legs in a roasting tin. Add the white wine, garlic, mustard seed, season lightly and mix well. Cover with foil and cook in the preheated oven for two hours.

Remove the roasting tin from the oven and leave to cool for 15 minutes. Pour off the fat into a container and set aside. Place the meat in a separate container and leave to cool until cool enough to handle

Remove the skin from the duck legs and finely chop. Shred the meat by hand making sure to remove all bones. Add all but 1 tbsp of the duck fat and season to taste. Mix well.

Place the rhubarb in a medium pan and add 1 tbsp of duck fat. Cook for two minutes until the rhubarb is soft. Add to the shredded meat and mix gently. Place the mixture in a terrine mould, pressing down with your hands. Place the terrine in the fridge for at least four hours.

Best served at room temperature with warm toast. It can be stored for up to a week.

Pan-Seared King Scallops with Black Pudding and Rhubarb

This is a simple and great dish from talented chef Tim Bilton, chef-owner of the Butchers Arms, Hepworth. In Tim's words, "the creaminess of the scallop the earthy richness of the black pudding and the sharpness of the rhubarb go perfectly well together."

Scallops can be bought in or out of their shells. Look out for scallops that have been harvested by hand-diving; this method has less impact on the environment than dredging for scallops.

Serves 4

> 6 sticks of Yorkshire forced rhubarb
> 50g sugar
> ½ orange, juice and zest
> ½ split vanilla pod
> Rapeseed oil
> 8 slices local black pudding
> 12 large scallops prepared and cleaned
> 50g Yorkshire butter
> Salt & pepper
> Herb oil and micro leaves for garnish

Wash the rhubarb then chop two sticks into batons, roughly chop the remaining four.

In a saucepan melt the sugar, orange juice and zest. Add the chopped rhubarb from the four sticks and vanilla, cover with a lid and simmer for 10–15 minutes. Remove the lid and blend until smooth, return back to the pan. Add the rhubarb batons and simmer a little faster for another five minutes. Set aside and keep warm.

In a frying pan heat a little rapeseed oil and add the black pudding.

Pan-Seared King Scallops with Black Pudding and Rhubarb.

Fry until crispy, turn over and repeat on the other side, remove from the pan and keep warm.

Place the cleaned, seasoned, scallops into the medium hot pan and sear in a little oil until golden brown. Turn over and add a knob of butter – this gives the scallops a rich creamy flavour. The scallops should be medium rare and warm in the middle. They should take about 5-6 minutes to cook – don't overcook.

Place the warm rhubarb onto the plate. Place the black pudding on the plate and neatly arrange the scallops on top. Drizzle with the garden herb oil and garnish with micro salad and more herbs.

Fennel and Rhubarb Chicken

Serves 4

1 tsp fennel seed, crushed	2 cloves garlic
1 tsp whole fennel seed	5 black peppercorns
4 tsp sea salt	1 bay leaf
¼ tsp chilli flakes	1 tsp coriander seeds
4 free-range chicken thighs, with bone and skin	1 small onion, thinly sliced
3 tbsp extra virgin olive oil	2 medium fennel bulbs, sliced into ½cm rings
375ml dry white wine	2 large stalks rhubarb, cut into 1cm pieces
235 ml cup water	Fresh herbs for garnish
3 tbsp honey	

Preheat oven to 190°C/ 375°F/Gas 5.

Mix together the crushed fennel seeds and chilli flakes with 1 tsp salt on a plate. Press each chicken thigh firmly into the seeds, turn and repeat on the other side.

Over a medium heat, heat 1 tsp of the olive oil in a heavy-bottomed pan. Cook the chicken thighs for three minutes on each side or until the skin is crispy – take extra care not to burn.

Put the pan into the preheated oven and roast the chicken for 10 – 12 minutes, remove from the oven and keep warm.

While the chicken is cooking, place the wine, water, honey, remaining salt, garlic, peppercorns , bay leaf and the whole fennel seeds and coriander in a large saucepan. Bring to a gentle boil, add the onion, fennel rings and remaining olive oil. Simmer for approx 10 mins or until the fennel is tender but not soft . Add the rhubarb and cook for a further 10 minutes.

Serve by dividing the vegetables between four serving plates, place the chicken on top and spoon a little of the sauce over. Garnish with fresh herbs.

Pan-fried Mackerel with Roasted Rhubarb

Serves 4

    4-5 stalks rhubarb
    1 tbsp light brown sugar
    2 fresh mackerel fillets
    4 tbsp plain flour, seasoned with salt and freshly ground
    black pepper
    Extra virgin olive oil
    2 sprigs fresh rosemary
    1 tbsp capers, drained

Preheat the oven to 200°C/400°F/Gas 6.

Cut the rhubarb into 15cm/6in lengths, place in a roasting tin with a few tbsp cold water and the sugar. Cover with foil and roast in the preheated oven until soft but still holding its shape. Cool, drain and reserve the juices.

Dip each mackerel fillet, skin side down, into the seasoned flour. Whilst holding the fillet, tap gently to remove any excess flour.

Heat the oil in a large frying pan. Place the fillets again, skin side down, into the hot pan, scatter over the rosemary. Cook on each side for two minutes, remove from the pan and keep warm. Add the rhubarb and the capers and warm through then remove and keep warm with the fish.

  Add a splash of the reserved rhubarb juices to the pan, stir vigorously to remove any bits from the bottom of the pan, cook for one minute. Serve immediately with the mackerel, the rhubarb and capers on the side.

Pan-fried Mackerel.

Rhubarb Relish.

Rhubarb Relish

Relish is similar, but not the same as a chutney. Both use sugar and vinegar as a preservative but the relish has less of both, and though it will keep for a few weeks in the refrigerator, it won't keep much longer.

Serve relish as a condiment of spicy sauce with fatty meats like pork and lamb, oily fish such as mackerel and salmon and it is also lovely with cheeses on a Ploughman's.

1 tbsp vegetable oil	2 tbsp light brown sugar
2 tbsp finely chopped shallot	250g rhubarb, washed, trimmed and chopped into small pieces
2 tbsp cider vinegar	
2 tbsp water	Salt and pepper

Place the oil into a roomy saucepan, add the shallot and cook for two minutes until softened but not browned. Add the vinegar and stir. Add the water and sugar and stir until the sugar has dissolved. Finally add the rhubarb, place a lid on the pan and cook gently for about 30 minutes or until the rhubarb is softened. Stir well. Season to taste.

Cool before serving. Store covered in the refrigerator for up to two weeks.

Lemon Spiced Rhubarb Chutney

2 unwaxed lemons, peeled and finely shredded and juiced	900g rhubarb, washed and cut into chunks
1in root ginger, lightly bruised	2 cloves garlic, gently crushed

450g sultanas	½ teaspoon cayenne
1kg soft, dark brown sugar	pepper
1 teaspoon mild curry	500ml organic cider
powder	vinegar

Tie the lemon peel and ginger into a small square of muslin.

Into a large pan, place the lemon juice, rhubarb chunks, sultanas, sugar, curry powder, cayenne pepper and vinegar. Add the muslin bag. Bring to a gentle boil and stir until the sugar dissolves.

Simmer for one hour until softened and thickened. Be careful not to burn the chutney, adjust the heat to make sure.

Remove the muslin bag. Fill sterilised jars, cover with wax paper and a lid. Will store in a dark, cool place for up to six months.

'Plopping Away' Rhubarb Chutney

Ann Smith, keeper of the 'Plopping Away' Rhubarb Chutney recipe, was a real character, known affectionately as Miss Marples, with her direct manner and keep-out-the-rain tweed hat! She was a really canny Yorkshire homemaker, as well as an all round great mum and grandmother.

This chutney recipe has travelled happily along the generations of the Smith family, with her granddaughters Annabel and Abigail carrying on the annual tradition of The Rhubarb Chutney making, following the lovely handwritten, now rather sticky, recipe card instructions!

As wife to her son Mike, I am an honoured sharer of the chutney making team. I look forward each year to using the rhubarb that was transferred from one garden to another, to keep the deemed to be circa 100 year old rhubarb on the go, and keeping the store cupboard topped up with chutney. **Irene Myers**

Rhubarb Chutney.

2lbs rhubarb	1 oz powdered ginger
2lbs sugar	1 onion – finely
1lb sultanas	chopped
1 pint vinegar	½ tsp cayenne pepper
1 oz salt	½ tsp ordinary pepper

Bring all the above to the boil. Reduce heat.

Let it plop away till thick and dark brown

Stir now and then. Pour into clean sterilised jars, put lid on and store. Has a long store cupboard life.

Roasted Rhubarb and Vanilla Crumble.

SWEET

Roasted Rhubarb and Vanilla Crumble

Rhubarb crumble is an all-time British food favourite. Traditionally the rhubarb would be stewed but in this recipe it is roasted in the oven with a little orange juice and vanilla. Roasting helps the rhubarb to keep its beautiful colour and also intensifies the flavour creating a delicious and memorable Roasted Rhubarb Crumble.

Serve with lashings of custard or vanilla ice cream.

Serves 4

450g rhubarb	*For the Crumble*
2 tbsp soft, brown sugar	115g cold butter
3 tbsp orange juice	170g all purpose/ plain
½ tsp vanilla extract	flour
	4 tbsp soft brown sugar

Preheat the oven to 175°C/350°F/Gas 4.

Cut the rhubarb into 3cm pieces. Place the rhubarb into an ovenproof dish. Sprinkle over the sugar. Mix the vanilla extract with the orange juice and pour over the rhubarb, loosely cover with tinfoil. Bake in the preheated oven for approx 20 minutes or until the rhubarb is cooked through but not falling apart.

Place all the crumble ingredients into a large baking bowl and roughly mash together to form lumpy crumbs. Don't worry about making the mixture even and fine, you are looking for a rustic looking topping.

Sprinkle the crumble loosely over the cooked rhubarb. Return the dish to the oven and cook for 30 - 35 minutes until the crumble is golden brown. Serve hot with custard sauce or vanilla ice cream.

You can also cook as individual puddings in ramekin dishes.

Caramelised Yorkshire Rhubarb, Ginger and Plums on Sweet Brioche Eggy Bread

A delicious and innovative recipe from talented Yorkshire chef Robert Ramsden. Robert works as a development chef with Delifresh, Bradford. He is a huge supporter of all local foods especially Yorkshire rhubarb.

Serves 4

200g diced butter
200g brown sugar
500g Yorkshire forced rhubarb, chopped into pieces
10g stem ginger, shredded
3 large plums, halved and stone removed

2 eggs
100ml milk
4 slices brioche
Black Pepper and Lavender Womersley Vinegar or Sloe Gin
4 tbsp clotted cream
1 lime

Heat a heavy bottomed frying pan and add half the diced butter. Once melted add the brown sugar and melt slowly until it becomes a caramel.

Add the rhubarb, ginger and plums and leave to cook in the caramel until the fruit is soft – about five minutes.

Heat another pan and add the remaining butter, gently whisk the eggs with the milk and dip the slices of brioche into the mixture. Pan fry in the butter until golden brown.

Place one slice of eggy bread on each of four plates, drizzle the vinegar into the caramel mix then place the rhubarb and plums on top of the bread and serve with a big dollop of clotted cream on each.

Garnish with rosemary or any herb flowers as desired.

Rhubarb and Sorrel Crisp

This unusual recipe comes from talented food writer Barbara Rolek who writes the About European Food website. It combines two ingredients Eastern Europeans love, sweet-tart flavour of rhubarb is married with the bite of young sorrel and topped with crunchy oats to make a surprisingly delicious, egg-free dessert. Young sorrel is perfect in this dish and strawberries can be substituted for part of the rhubarb, if desired.

12 portions

For the filling:	Crust and Topping:
4 large stalks of rhubarb, finely chopped	200g plain flour
2 cups finely chopped sorrel	200g cups rolled oats
1 tbsp orange zest	150g cup soft brown sugar
1 tsp vanilla extract	½ tsp alt
60ml water	½ tsp cinnamon
3 tbsp cornflour	75g chopped nuts (optional)
	170g cold butter

Preheat the oven to 175 °C/350 °F/Gas 4.

Lightly grease a 33x 23cm/13x9in ovenproof dish. In a large saucepan, mix together rhubarb, sorrel, zest and vanilla. Bring to a boil over medium-high heat, reduce and cook, stirring frequently, for 4 minutes. In a small bowl, dissolve corn flour in ¼ cup water. Stir into rhubarb mixture and cook until thickened, stirring constantly. Set aside to cool slightly.

In a medium bowl, mix together flour, oats, brown sugar, salt, cinnamon and nuts (if using). Cut in butter until finely crumbled. Put three cups of mixture into the bottom of the prepared baking pan, pressing to make an even layer.

Pour slightly cooled rhubarb over crust, spreading evenly. Sprinkle with remaining crumb mixture. Place pan on a baking sheet to catch any drips and bake 30-40 minutes or until golden and bubbly. Cut into squares while still warm, but not hot.

Serve with vanilla ice cream or custard.

Rhubarb and Sorrel Crisp.

Rhubarb Crumble Truffles

Fiona Sciolti, is an Artisan Chocolatier in North Lincolnshire. She combines her Italian passion with her love of quintessentially English country flavours to make beautiful, award winning botanical chocolates, using natural and local ingredients.

Fiona says these truffles are lovely as a gift or served after a meal, but remember that a little goes a long way, as these are very rich.

This recipe makes approx. 30- 40 truffles.

> *For the Crumble*
> 50g butter
> 80g plain flour
> 40g demerara sugar
> 35g chopped flaked almonds
>
> *For the Rhubarb Chocolate Truffle*
> 50g rhubarb jam
> 50g butter, softened
> 130g white chocolate
> 20g finely chopped candied peel
> 1 level tsp mixed spice
> Freshly ground black pepper

To make the Crumble:

Pre-heat the oven to 200°C/400°F/Gas Mark 6.

Lightly rub the butter into flour until the mixture resembles fine breadcrumbs. Add the demerara and almonds and gently mix together. Sprinkle on to a baking tray and bake for 15-20 minutes until golden. Set aside and leave to go completely cold.

Chocolate Truffle Mixture:

In a new bowl beat up the rhubarb jam and butter until light, pale and fluffy. Make sure your butter is very soft; however it's important not to melt the butter as it will alter the texture of your chocolates. In another bowl melt your chocolate over a pan of simmering water, stirring until fully melted. Take off and let cool, but make sure the chocolate remains melted. Beat into the butter and jam mixture, add the peel, mixed spice and freshly ground black pepper. Cover and refrigerate.

Finishing:

Spread the crumble mixture into a shallow bowl, breaking any clumps with your fingers. Take the chocolate truffle mixture from the fridge and, using a teaspoon, scoop out small amounts of the mixture. With clean hands, shape the mixture into balls and drop them into the crumble. Roll and press firmly into the crumble until they are coated. Place on a clean plate and continue with the mixture until it is all used up.

Alternatively, for a hard chocolate outer shell you can dip them in melted chocolate and then sprinkle with the crumble mixture.

These truffles are best served cold, so cling film your finished chocolates and keep in the fridge for up to two days until ready to serve.

"Throughout my life my rhubarb has come to me via my dad and his beloved allotment. A magical childhood playground with robins' nests in the shed, my own little plot and where the fairies would come and visit. They would invisibly fly by and leave me sweeties tied from the apple trees, scattered on the straw bales or hidden amongst the rhubarb. The rhubarb was always a fascination – watching those first buds come through and each visit the shoots would have magically grown. My dad is now eighty and still visits his beloved allotment almost every day.' **Fiona Sciolti**

Rhubarb Crumble Truffles.

Rhubarb and Sweet Cicely Pie.

Rhubarb and Sweet Cicely Pie

Sweet Cicely has a gentle aniseed flavour and is a wonderful, underused herb which complements rhubarb perfectly. Alison Dodd grows Sweet Cicely herb from her own business, Herbs Unlimited, Sandhutton near Thirsk, North Yorkshire and brings you this great tasting way to eat your rhubarb.

Pastry for the Pie:

480g plain flour
200g margarine (you will also need 5g margarine to grease the pie mould)
1 tsp ground ginger
20g caster sugar
2 medium size free-range eggs, cracked and beaten together
Splash of iced cold water to bind (if necessary)
Zest of 1 lemon

Preheat the oven to 180°C/375°F/Gas 5.

Using a large bowl sieve the flour and powdered ginger into the bowl.

Place the margarine in small cubes and using your fingertips rub the mixture together until it forms a sand-like consistency. Add the sugar.

Add the beaten eggs and, using a wooden spoon, stir into the pastry with the lemon zest until all the ingredients are mixed in. Add a splash of iced water to help bind if necessary.

Wrap in cling film and allow to rest in the fridge for 20 minutes.

Pie filling:

1.5kg chopped rhubarb (see note at the end)
250g golden light brown sugar

Juice of 1 lemon
1 tbsp cornflour
7 stems of sweet cicely with the leaves removed from the stems, washed and gently patted dry on a clean tea towel. Chop these leaves with scissors or a knife.

To cook the rhubarb place the washed chopped stems of rhubarb into a large pan. Sprinkle the golden light brown sugar, add the lemon juice, cover the pan with a lid and cook on a gentle heat until the rhubarb has softened, about 5 minutes.

Place 1 tsp cornflour in a small dish mix with 1 tsp cold water and mix well.

Pour this mixture into the boiling rhubarb and stir with a wooden spoon until all incorporated. A 'gluepy' mix is what you are looking for.

Pour the mixture onto a tray or dish and cool for 10 minutes. When cool add the chopped leaves of sweet cicely to the pie mix.

Line the buttered pie dish with two-thirds of the sweet pastry. Fill the pie with the sweet cicely rhubarb mixture and brush the edge of the pie with a little beaten egg, mixed with water. Roll out the remaining pastry to create the pie lid, cut to shape then crimp the edge.

Brush the pie with more egg wash and sprinkle with sugar before baking to give a caramel crunchy top to your pie.

Bake in the preheated oven for 30 minutes until golden brown and cooked.

Rest briefly before slicing and serve with custard, cream, or ice cream and a sprig of sweet cicely to garnish.

Note: Try to use the coloured part of the rhubarb and leave the greener parts of the stems for chutneys and jams. Alternatively you can use indoor forced rhubarb.

Assiette of Rhubarb

Rhubarb Cheesecake ~ Rhubarb Syrup ~ Ginger Crunch Ice Cream ~ Rhubarb Jelly ~ Pannacotta ~ Chocolate Marquise

by Chef Stephanie Moon.

Stephanie is consultant chef at Rudding Park Hotel, Harrogate and a passionate supporter of Yorkshire Rhubarb. Watch rhubarb evolve into six delicous, sophisticated desserts in her talented hands.

Serves 6

Rhubarb Cheesecake

100g ginger nut biscuits	4g gelatine sheets soaked in cold water
40g unsalted butter, melted	
70g rhubarb	90g cream cheese
80g sugar	90g sour cream
	90g whipped cream

Break the biscuits to a crumb by placing them in a bag and beating with a rolling pin. Add the melted butter, mix and then press into the base of four individual round moulds

Chop the rhubarb into chunks and place in a pan with 2 tablespoons water and 20g sugar. Heat for approximately 5 minutes until very soft. Add the drained, soaked gelatine, mix and leave to cool.

Beat the cheese, remaining sugar and sour cream until smooth, add the stewed rhubarb. When the mix is cool fold in the whipped cream and set in the prepared moulds on top of the biscuit base.

Assiette of Rhubarb.

Rhubarb Syrup

100ml water   200g sugar   100g chopped rhubarb

Boil the water and sugar for 5 minutes then add the chopped rhubarb. Simmer for 5 minutes, remove from the heat and pass through a fine sieve.

The syrup should be sticky so cook for a further few minutes if necessary.

Cool and then pour on top of the cheesecake before the syrup sets.

Ginger Crunch Ice Cream

400ml double cream
½ split vanilla pod
6 egg yolks
100g sugar

¼ packet ginger biscuits,
roughly crushed
100g condensed milk

Boil the cream, condensed milk and vanilla pod. Scratch out the seeds using the back of a knife and add the seeds to the milk. Pour onto the creamed egg yolks and sugar.

Return back to the pan on a low heat stirring continuously until the mixture coats the back of the spoon. Remove from the pan and sieve out the vanilla pod chill. Churn and freeze until it is an ice cream consistency add the crushed ginger nut biscuits and freeze until required.

Rhubarb Jelly

½ pint stock syrup
(½ pint water and 100g
castor sugar, boiled
together)

2 sticks of rhubarb,
chopped
8 leaves gelatine

Heat the ingredients for the stock syrup and add the rhubarb, bring to the boil. Once the rhubarb is soft, sieve and reserve the chunks of rhubarb for the pannacotta recipe.

Soak the gelatine in cold water, when soft squeeze dry and add to the above jelly mix until all the gelatine is dissolved. Pour the mix into 4 individual moulds and set in the fridge for approx 2 hours.

Pannacotta

¼ pint of milk
80g mascarpone
cheese

1 large plump vanilla
pod, split
1 sheet of gelatine

Boil the milk with the split vanilla pod dispersing the seeds throughout the milk. Once it has boiled take off the heat.

Soak the gelatine leaf in cold water and when soft, squeeze dry.

Add to the milk and mix in with a wooden spoon until melted. Remove the vanilla pod.

Next whisk in the mascarpone and allow it to set until sloppy in the fridge.

Spoon a little of the reserved rhubarb compote from the jellies into 4 shot glasses then pour over the pannacotta.

Chocolate Marquise

4 free range egg yolks
100g caster sugar
110g quality dark chocolate
130g unsalted butter cut into chunks about the size of a dice.
40g good quality cocoa powder
Seeds of ½ vanilla pod split
300ml double cream
Rhubarb compote to top the marquise (use the left over from making the jelly)

Line the terrine mould with cling film, leaving the excess to hang over the sides.

Use an electric mixer, mix the egg yolks and sugar in a Pyrex bowl until well combined. Place the bowl over a pan of simmering water – the base of the bowl must not touch the boiling water as it will curdle the mix. Add the chocolate and whisk for 5-6 minutes until melted. Add the butter one piece at a time, whisking each piece in well until it melts. Allow to cool for five minutes then fold in cocoa powder.

Beat the cream and vanilla seeds until it forms soft peaks. Fold into the chocolate mix, ideally half first then the other half, until all mixed in. Pour into terrine mould, fold over cling film to cover, and then place in the fridge for 4/6 hours if possible.

Turn out terrine by placing under a hot water tap and the terrine will dislodge itself. Remove the cling film and slice. decorate with compote.

Rhubarb and Champagne Jelly

This recipe is a quick and simple, yet sophisticated dessert. Though rhubarb is more often thought of as an ingredient of 'nursery food' in puddings, here it shines as a delicate jelly with Champagne. This recipe is adapted from Mrs Beeton's recipe for Rhubarb Jelly from her famous tome, Mrs Beeton's Book of Household Management.

Serves 4

> 750g fresh rhubarb, washed, cut into 2cm chunks
> 110g fine sugar
> 1 litre water
> 250 ml Champagne
> 10g or 6 sheets gelatine, soaked in a little warm water

Place the rhubarb in a non-aluminum pan, add the sugar and water and bring gently to the boil. Simmer for 20 minutes then remove from the heat and leave until completely cold.

Pour the rhubarb into a fine sieve set over a large bowl. Leave the juice to drip for 10 minutes. Do not force the rhubarb through. Measure 500ml/1 pint of the strained juice and place into a small pan.

Dissolve the powdered gelatine in 3 tbsp water – if using leaf gelatine, remove from the warm water with your fingers gently squeezing away any excess water.

Add the gelatine to the rhubarb juice in the pan and heat gently until the gelatine is completely dissolved. DO NOT BOIL. Leave to cool for 10 minute then add the Champagne and mix gently.

Divide between four glasses and chill for at least four hours.

Serve with Amoretti or tiny biscuits. The cooked rhubarb can be used in a pie or a crumble.

Rhubarb and Champagne Jelly.

Ginger Burnt Cream with Stewed Rhubarb and East Yorkshire Sugar Cakes

See what happens to rhubarb in the hands of a Michelin-starred Chef.

James Mackenzie is Chef-Proprietor of the renowned Pipe and Glass Inn, South Dalton. The Sugar Cakes are deceptively named as they are more biscuit like. The original recipe dates back over 200 years and came to light in 2007 in the Beverley archives department of the town council when it was moving to its new building. When asked by the BBC for his opinion on the recipe, James tested it and found it too strong for modern tatse because of the large quantity of cloves and mace and so adapted the recipe. It is a perfect accompaniment to rhubarb.

Serves 4

Rhubarb
4 sticks of rhubarb
150g caster sugar

East Yorkshire Sugar Cakes
680g plain flour
225g caster sugar
450g butter, melted
25g mixed spice
25g ground nutmeg
½ tsp ground cloves

Burnt cream mix
350ml double cream
125ml milk
5 egg yolks
75g caster sugar
2tbsp grated root ginger

Preheat the oven to 175 °C/350 °F/Gas 4.

First make the cakes: Put all ingredients into a bowl and mix together. Lay cling film on a board, lay the cake dough and roll up in the cling film to form a sausage shape and place in the refrigerator for the dough to firm up.

Remove from the refrigerator, slice and lay on a greased baking sheet. Bake in the preheated oven for 10 minutes.

To stew the rhubarb: Chop the sticks of rhubarb into 3cm lengths, place on a baking tray. Sprinkle over the sugar and a little water, cover with foil and bake in the oven for about 10 -12 minutes until just cooked. Remove from the oven and leave to cool in the tray. This way the rhubarb will keep its shape.

Reduce the temperature of the oven to 160 °C/325 °F/ Gas 3.

For the burnt cream: Mix the egg yolks with the sugar in a bowl. Boil the milk and cream in a pan with the ginger. Remove from the heat and leave the ginger to infuse the flavour for a few minutes then strain through a sieve over the egg mix whisking thoroughly. Pour into individual ovenproof dishes (3in x 2in deep, or 5in x 1in).

Place the dishes into a deep oven-tray and pour in water to come a third of the way up the dishes. Bake in the oven at 160°C for half an hour to 40 minutes.

Remove from the oven and set in the fridge.

When ready to serve, evenly sprinkle the surface of the brulée with a thin layer of caster sugar and blow torch, or place under a hot grill, until golden brown. Repeat until you have a thick, golden and hard surface.

Ginger Burnt Cream with Stewed Rhubarb and
East Yorkshire Sugar Cakes.

The Radio

During radio programmes of the 1920s and 1930s, the background
noise for crowd scenes was often achieved by a moderately large
group of people mumbling 'rhubarb' under their breath with random
inflections.

Rhubarb Radio is an internet station based at The Custard Factory in
Birmingham, UK, hosting a range of shows and programming
representing West Midlands arts and music and available worldwide.

Chef Brian Turner's
Yorkshire Rhubarb Mess

'It was my privilege to be brought up in the market town of Morley until I left age 17. I have great memories of life as a youngster and from where we lived we could see the hills round East Ardsley, famous as part of the Yorkshire rhubarb triangle. As far as I am concerned Yorkshire rhubarb was, is and will always be the best in the world. I left Morley and have lived in London ever since and have been lucky enough to visit some pretty posh places, Henley, Wimbledon and of course Eton College. This recipe combines all those memories and experiences – it's simple and delicious to eat.' **Chef Brian Turner CBE**

Serves 4

> 6oz rhubarb coulis
> 8oz poached rhubarb
> ¾ pt. whipped crème Chantilly
> 8oz meringues
> Rhubarb to decorate

Put coulis in bottom of martini glass. Break up meringues and mix with half of the cream, and half the poached rhubarb, put some in each glass above the coulis.

Lay rhubarb on top, then cream and meringue on top of this. Skim with a little whipped crème Chantilly and pipe a rosette on top.

Meanwhile keep the cooking liquor for the rhubarb and reduce to a syrup on a high heat. Remove from the heat and cool.

Decorate the rosette with poached rhubarb and sprinkle with the reduced juice.

Rhubarb Pavlova

This dish has the potential to look a right mess as it all slides about, but don't worry – it's incredibly delicious.

Serves 4

For the Meringue:
4 fresh egg whites
250g soft brown sugar
1 tsp cornflour
1 tsp white wine vinegar
A few drops of vanilla extract
For the Compote:
450g fresh rhubarb, washed, cut into 4cm pieces
150g caster sugar

200ml water
Zest & juice of 2 oranges:

For the Custard:
4 egg yolks
1 tbsp caster sugar
1 tsp cornflour
300ml single cream
Few drops vanilla extract
200ml whipping cream

Preheat the oven to 120°C / 250°F /Gas ½.

Whisk the egg whites until just stiff, then gradually add the sugar a little at a time, whisking continuously until stiff, then gently fold in the remaining ingredients.

Line a baking tray with baking parchment. Shape the meringue mix either into a large circle or six smaller individual ones. Place in a preheated oven for an hour and a half until firm. Switch off the oven and leave the meringue inside for another 30 minutes.

Place the rhubarb in an ovenproof dish. Turn the oven on to 160°C / 320°F / gas 5.

Place the remaining ingredients in a saucepan, bring up to a simmer and pour over the rhubarb. Cover the dish with foil and bake for 15-20 minutes. Do not overcook. Set aside the rhubarb to cool.

Next, make the custard. Whisk the egg yolks with the sugar and cornflour in a large bowl. Heat the cream and vanilla in a small saucepan. Just as the cream is about to boil, pour over the egg yolk mixture and whisk thoroughly. Return the mixture to the pan and cook over a low heat until thickened, then set aside to cool.

To finish the dish, whip the cream until soft peaks form. Top the meringue with the whipped cream, drizzle over the custard and place the rhubarb on the top, along with a drizzle of its juice.

Rhubarb and Vanilla Jam

700g rhubarb, washed and roughly chopped
700g jam sugar
1 vanilla pod, split lengthways
juice of 1 orange

140°C/275°F/Gas 1.

In a heavy-based pan, or jam pan put the rhubarb, sugar, vanilla and orange juice. Heat gently and stir until all the sugar has dissolved. Slowly increase the heat to bring the jam up to a rolling boil. Boil hard for 10 minutes taking care to make sure the bottom of the pan doesn't burn.

To test if the jam is set: Place a saucer in the freezer for 10 minutes while the jam is boiling. Once the jam has boiled put one tsp of the jam onto the chilled saucer, leave for one minute. Gently push the jam with your finger to see if the surface wrinkles. If it does, the jam is set, if not continue to cook for a few minutes and repeat until ready.

Once ready, skin any scum from the surface, remove the vanilla pod and rest the jam for 10 minutes. Pour the jam into hot, sterilised jars – see the note below. Cover with either a lid or cellophane and leave to cool.

To sterilise the jars, heat in a warm oven until hot but not scalding or run on a hot rinse in the dishwasher.

Rhubarb Fool

A deliciously simple way to serve young, sweet, forced rhubarb.

Serves 4

> 400g forced rhubarb, cut into 1cm pieces
> 75g clear honey
> 150g mascarpone
> 250ml whipping cream

Place the rhubarb in a saucepan with the honey. Cook gently for 20 minutes until a soft pulp. Leave to cool. Reserve 4 dessertspoons of the pulp.

Rhubarb Fool.

Rhubarb Fool.

Beat the mascarpone in a bowl until smooth and loose, then stir in the rhubarb. Do not overstir, the cream should have a marbled effect. Whip the cream to soft peaks, then fold into the rhubarb mix.

Serve in glasses with the rhubarb pulp on top. Goes really well with a ginger biscuit or a small piece of parkin.

Rhubarb and Custard Crumble Tart

A clever and delicious crossover between a pie and a crumble

170g plain flour
110g chilled butter, cubed
55g light muscavado sugar
2 large free range eggs plus 3 egg yolks
120g caster sugar
1 tbsp cornflour
300ml double cream
2 vanilla pods, split lengthways, seeds scraped and reserved
500g rhubarb cut into 4cm lengths
Knob of butter
500g ready made sweet shortcrust pastry

Preheat the oven to 200 °C/400°F/Gas 6.

Put a baking sheet in the oven as it heats up.

To make the crumble put the flour and butter together with a pinch of salt into a large mixing bowl. Rub together until the mixture resembles coarse sand. Stir in the sugar, then scatter over a shallow baking tray. Keep to one side.

Roll out the pastry on a floured work surface, and line a greased 21cm x 3.5cm deep loose bottom tart tin. Prick all over with a fork. Line the tart case with baking paper and fill with baking beans or rice. Bake for 12 minutes on the hot baking sheet. Remove the paper and beans or rice, bake for a further 5 minutes or until the pastry is crisp but not too brown. Remove from the oven and set aside. Leave the oven on.

Prepare the custard by mixing the eggs, egg yolks and half the caster sugar and cornflour in a bowl. Put the cream, a split vanilla pod plus the seeds into a pan over a medium heat, bring almost to a boil. Gently pour over the egg mixture, whisking constantly.

Pour back into the pan and heat until the custard thickens. Leave to cool.

Place the rhubarb into a bowl, add the remaining sugar, and the seeds of the remaining vanilla pod. Scatter over a shallow baking tray, dot the top with butter and drizzle with a tbsp water then add the vanilla pod. Bake for 15 minutes.

Strain the rhubarb and reserve the juices.

Pour the custard into the pastry case, cover with the roasted rhubarb and gently push down. Place onto the baking sheet for 12 to 15 minutes or until the custard is just set. Sprinkle with the crumble onto another baking sheet and cook in the oven alongside the tart until crunchy and golden. Remove both from the oven. Remove the tart from the tin, sprinkle over the crumble and serve with the reserved rhubarb juices.

Rhubarb Festival

There are few vegetables that can claim to have a whole festival dedicated to them. Rhubarb has several around the world, with the most famous being the Wakefield Festival of Rhubarb. The event is organised by Wakefield Council and is held in February every year. Wakefield has traditional links with growing rhubarb and is part of the famous 'Rhubarb Triangle'. The three-day festival celebrates these links. It is also a showcase for other regional produce and talented local chefs. There are cookery demonstrations, a food market, walking tours and visits to rhubarb growers.

Rhubarb and Honey Ice Cream

This ice cream recipe uses crème fraiche – a lightly acidulated cream. It gives a lovely tang to match the rhubarb, which then balances with the sweetness of the honey. If you don't have an ice cream machine, don't worry; this recipe uses liquid glucose. which helps to create a smooth ice cream and prevents crystallisation so can be made without a machine. Just follow the directions below.

Serve 4

> 100g fine or caster sugar
> 500 ml milk
> 3 tsp liquid glucose
> 3 large egg yolks
> 250g crème fraiche
> ¼ pt/ 150ml whipping cream
> 3 tbsp stewed rhubarb– see page 42
> 1 tbsp runny honey

Place the sugar, milk and liquid glucose into a large saucepan and stir well. Place over a gentle heat and warm the milk through until it is slightly steaming but not boiling.

Whisk the egg yolks in a roomy baking bowl until light and fluffy. Whisking continuously, slowly add the warmed milk. Return the egg and milk mixture back into the pan and whisk thoroughly.

Heat gently,constantly stirring until the cream has thickened. Do not allow the cream to boil; if you feel it is cooking too quickly, or sticking to the bottom of the pan, remove it from the heat to allow it to cool a little, lower the heat then continue cooking. The more time you take over this part the better the cream will be in the end.

Strain the cream through a fine sieve and put to one side and allow to cool.

Once the custard base is cool, add the crème fraiche, the whipping cream, rhubarb and honey. Stir well. Either churn in an ice cream machine or pour the mixture into a shallow freezer container and place in the freezer. Beat the mixture three or four times as it freezes to break up any ice crystals and to create a smooth ice cream.

Once frozen, cover and store until needed. Remove the ice cream from the freezer fifteen minutes before serving to soften it a little.

Serve drizzled with a little more honey if desired.

Code Name 'Rhubarb'
Used in RAF operations when sections of fighters or fighter-bombers, taking full advantage of low cloud and poor visibility, would cross the English Channel. They would then drop below cloud level to search for opportunity targets such as railway locomotives and rolling stock, aircraft on the ground, enemy troops and vehicles on roads.

DRINKS

Rhubarb Schnapps

*by **Chef Andrew Pern**, The Star at Harome*

2kg of rhubarb, roughly chopped
1kg granulated sugar
1.5 litres of vodka or other preferred alcohol

First of the season forced Yorkshire rhubarb is the best; its vibrant pink hue gives a lovely glow. Stew down the rhubarb with a little splash of water, place a lid on top and cook for 10 to 15 minutes. Strain the juice from the pulp through a fine sieve – set the fruit aside and use for a compôte.

Add the vodka and sugar to the juice, mix thoroughly and pour into a large bottle or another suitable vessel.

For the first few days tip and turn the bottles to ensure all the sugar is dissolved, then store out of sunlight and out of harm's way!

Do not drink until approx 6 weeks at the earliest.

Rhubarb Wine

This recipe comes from Marjorie Greetham. Both she and her mother before her used to make this wine recipe before and after the war – they also made ginger beer but the bottles kept exploding! She was a great Yorkshire cook and made use of any 'free' food, including the patch in the garden with rhubarb. Back then 'real' wine was a luxury only the elite could afford.

5 lbs rhubarb	½ oz isinglass
4 lbs sugar	1 gallon of cold water
1 lemon	

Cut rhubarb into small pieces and put into earthenware crock, bowl or cruise. Pour cold water over and let it stand for three days. Stir occasionally each day. Strain and add sugar. Stir until it dissolves. Add rind and juice of lemon.

Dissolve isinglass in a little hot water. Add to liquor and stand for six days. Skim off crust and strain. Put into bottles and, after a fortnight, cork them (not screw tops). Ready for use in six weeks.

If isinglass is not obtainable, I use beaten whites of three eggs per gallon.

Rhubarb and Strawberry Cordial

This is the perfect drink for a warm, summer's day. It makes the most of the seasonal fruits with an added hint of rose.

340g ripe strawberries, roughly chopped
4 sticks of rhubarb, roughly chopped
340g caster sugar
1 litre water
1 tbsp rose syrup

Using a heavy based saucepan, place the fruit and sugar over a low heat, stir gently and heat through until the sugar has melted and the fruit begins to soften and release its juices.

Add the water. Continue to cook over a medium heat (NOT boiling) for 15 minutes, remove from the heat and cool completely. Pass through a fine sieve, pressing down to collect all the juice, add the rose syrup. Store in the refrigerator. To serve, dilute with either still or sparkling water.

Rhubarb Schnapps.

Rhubarb and Strawberry Cordial.

Recommendations for all things Rhubarb

Yorkshire Rhubarb Growers holding Protected Designation of Origin (PDO) status

E Oldroyd & Sons, Hopefield Farm, The Shutts, Leadwell Lane, Rothwell, Leeds

John Dobson & Son (Greenfield Produce), Carlton, Wakefield

D.Westwood & Son, Thorpe, Wakefield

D.Tomlinson, Pudsey, Leeds

Gardens

RHS Garden, Wisley, Woking, Surrey, GU23 6QB

RHS Garden, Harlow Carr, Crag Lane, Harrogate, North Yorkshire, HG3 1QB

Clumber Park, Worksop, Nottinghamshire, S80 3AZ

The Alnwick Garden, Denwick Lane, Alnwick, Northumberland, NE66 1YU

Eden Project, Bodelva, Cornwall, PL24 2SG

Photo Credits